The Battle of Gaugamela: The History of Alexan Victory and the Destruction of the Achaeme

By Charles River Editors

The Battle of Gaugamela by Jan Brueghel the Elder

About Charles River Editors

Charles River Editors is a boutique digital publishing company, specializing in bringing history back to life with educational and engaging books on a wide range of topics. Keep up to date with our new and free offerings with this 5 second sign up on our weekly mailing list, and visit Our Kindle Author Page to see other recently published Kindle titles.

We make these books for you and always want to know our readers' opinions, so we encourage you to leave reviews and look forward to publishing new and exciting titles each week.

Introduction

Andrew Dunn's picture of an ancient bust of Alexander

"Then the Scythian cavalry rode along the line, and came into conflict with the front men of Alexander's array, but he nevertheless still continued to march towards the right, and almost entirely got beyond the ground which had been cleared and levelled by the Persians. Then Darius, fearing that his chariots would become useless, if the Macedonians advanced into the uneven ground, ordered the front ranks of his left wing to ride round the right wing of the Macedonians, where Alexander was commanding, to prevent him from marching his wing any further. This being done, Alexander ordered the cavalry of the Grecian mercenaries under the command of Menidas to attack them. But the Scythian cavalry and the Bactrians, who had been drawn up with them, sallied forth against them and being much more numerous they put the small body of Greeks to rout. Alexander then ordered Aristo at the head of the Paeonians and Grecian auxiliaries to attack the Scythians, and the barbarians gave way. But the rest of the Bactrians, drawing near to the Paeonians and Grecian auxiliaries, caused their own comrades who were already in flight to turn and renew the battle; and thus they brought about a general cavalry engagement, in which more of Alexander's men fell, not only being overwhelmed by the multitude of the barbarians, but also because the Scythians themselves and their horses were much more completely protected with armour for guarding their bodies. Notwithstanding this, the Macedonians sustained their assaults, and assailing them violently squadron by squadron, they succeeded in pushing them out of rank." - Arrian

At one point in antiquity, the Achaemenid Persian Empire was the largest empire the world had ever seen, but aside from its role in the Greco-Persian Wars and its collapse at the hands of Alexander the Great, it has been mostly overlooked. When it has been studied, the historical sources have mostly been Greek, the very people the Persians sought to conquer. Needless to say, their versions were biased, and attitudes about the Persians were only exacerbated by Alexander the Great and his biographers, who maintained a fiery hatred toward Xerxes I of Persia due to his burning of Athens. The Macedonians targeted many of his building projects after their capture of Persepolis, and they pushed an even bleaker picture of the king, one of an idle, indolent, cowardly, and corrupt ruler. It was not until excavations in the region during the 20th century that many of the relics, reliefs, and clay tablets that offer so much information about Persian life could be studied for the first time. Through archaeological remains, ancient texts, and work by a new generation of historians, a picture can today be built of this remarkable civilization and their most famous leaders.

Of course, far more is known about Alexander the Great and his military accomplishments, the most important of which was bringing about the demise of the Persian Empire. Over the last 2,000 years, ambitious men have dreamed of forging vast empires and attaining eternal glory in battle, but of all the conquerors who took steps toward such dreams, none were ever as successful as antiquity's first great conqueror. Leaders of the 20th century hoped to rival Napoleon's accomplishments, while Napoleon aimed to emulate the accomplishments of Julius Caesar. But Caesar himself found inspiration in Alexander the Great (356-323 BCE), the Macedonian king who managed to stretch an empire from Greece to the Himalayas in Asia by the age of 30. It took less than 15 years for Alexander to conquer much of the known world.

Ever since the famous Persian invasions that had been repelled by the Athenians at Marathon and then by the Spartans at Thermopylae and Plataea, Greece and Persia had been at odds. For the past few years they had enjoyed an uneasy peace, but that peace was shattered when, in 334 BCE, Alexander crossed the Hellespont into Persia. He brought with him an army of 50,000 infantry, 6,000 cavalry and a navy of over 100 ships, a mixed force of Macedonians, Greeks, Thracians and Illyrians, all chosen for their specific strengths (the Thessalians, for example, were famous cavalrymen). He was still just 22.

Darius III, king of Persia at the time of Alexander's invasion, was no tactical genius, but he was an intelligent and persistent enemy who had been handed the throne just before the arrival of the indomitable Alexander. His misfortune was to face an enemy at the forefront of military innovation and flexibility, a fighting force that he was not equipped to handle, and the unconquerable will of the Macedonian army, fueled by devotion to their daring and charismatic king. He would personally face Alexander twice, once at the Battle of Issus and again at the Battle of Gaugamela, with the latter conflict deciding the fate of the Western world.

The Battle of Gaugamela: The History of Alexander the Great's Decisive Victory and the Destruction of the Achaemenid Persian Empire looks at one of antiquity's most important conflicts, and the profound ramifications of Alexander's campaign. Along with pictures depicting important people, places, and events, you will learn about the battle like never before.

The Battle of Gaugamela: The History of Alexander the Great's Decisive Victory and the Destruction of the Achaemenid Persian Empire

The Rise of Alexander

"How great are the dangers I face to win a good name in Athens." – attributed to Alexander

Traditionally speaking, although the Macedonians spoke a dialect of Greek and were virtually identical to the Greeks in many of their customs and culture, the Greeks of the more prominent city-states generally considered the Macedonians to be borderline barbarians.

When the Macedonian King Philip II had come to power in 360 BCE, he was only 23 and had spent most of his adult life as the hostage of an Illyrian tribe (King, 2018, p. 70). Philip II's ascension to the Macedonian throne took place in the midst of great chaos in Macedonia, with the Illyrians continually raiding the kingdom from the north while other Greeks took advantage of this by taking even more Macedonian land. The problem was further exacerbated by Athenian attempts to influence the throne.

King Philip II of Macedon

Nonetheless, in about five years, Philip II not only brought order back to Macedon but also the respect it had once earned from Greek and non-Greek neighbors alike. Philip was also able to take further advantage of the deteriorating political situation in mainland Greece. The Peloponnesian War was supposed to settle the difference between the Greek city-states once and for all. It was thought the victor would impose its will over the Greeks to institute a Pan-Hellenic state under one government, or at least a federated form of government. Although the Spartans attempted to do so after their victory in the war, their resources and manpower were too depleted to impose any type of lasting hegemony over the other Greeks.

In 370 BCE, Sparta attempted to preserve a toehold of influence in Arkadia by invading, but the Arkadians, knowing which way the wind blew, promptly asked for assistance from Thebes. A Theban army under Epaminondas was promptly sent to the Arkadians' aid and, after having liberated the region, began marching toward Sparta proper. For reasons unknown, Epaminondas decided not to march toward the city itself, perhaps realizing that such an unprecedented threat to their very city would drive the Spartans to feats of Herculean desperation. Instead, he diverted his army toward the helot capital of Messene and began liberating vast tracts of Messenia, ensuring an all-out helot uprising and then fortifying the city so the Spartans could not retake it.

Though Thebes had long been an important city, it had never been predominant militarily. Once it did, however, the main city-states of Greece now turned against Thebes. Worried by the newly ascendant power of Thebes, several of Sparta's erstwhile enemies, including Mantinea and Athens, made common cause with the Spartans. In 362 the Boeotian League, led by Theban forces, faced this impromptu coalition at the Battle of Mantinea. Though the Spartans were once again defeated, Epaminondas himself was killed in the hour of victory. A peace was sought, but Sparta snubbed the negotiations, which decreed Messenia independent. Hemmed in by enemies – Argos, Messenia, Arkadia – on all sides, Sparta was in no position to pursue imperialistic policies, and indeed the city's very survival was threatened.

A semblance of balance was established, with each of the great city-states, Athens included, sitting back and catching their breath. For several years it even seemed as though peace might be an option, but just outside the borders of Greece, Philip ambitiously seized on an opportunity.

By the year 352 BCE, Philip II believed Macedon could potentially be the power to unify the entire Hellenic world, so he began his campaign to forcefully unite the Hellenic world by sending his modern army west into Thrace and south into Thessaly. The Thessalians were having problems with the other Greeks, particularly the Phocians, and they formed the Thessalian League to combat central Greek aggression. Knowing the Macedonians were experiencing a military renaissance, hoping to secure their northern border, the Thessalians not only invited Philip II and the Macedonians to join the Thessalian League, but they also made the Macedonian king the *archon* or general of the league's military forces (King, 2018, p. 78). Philip II upheld his end of the deal by driving the Phocians from Thessaly. Diodorus wrote that "in response to a summons from the Thessalians [, Philip] entered Thessaly with his army, and at first carried on a war against Lycophron, tyrant of Pherae, in support of the Thessalians; but later, when Lycophron summoned an auxiliary force from his allies the Phocians, Phayllus, the brother of Onomarchus, was dispatched with seven thousand men. But Philip defeated the Phocians and drove them out of Thessaly." (Diodorus, *Library of History*, XVI, 35).

With Macedonia's southern border secured and the Illyrians and Thracians pacified for the most part, Philip II turned his attention to the Chalcidic League, which had always been problematic so far as Macedonia's quest for hegemony in northern Greece was concerned. The city-states of the league were descended from Athenian colonists and held ideas in opposition to the Macedonian monarchy. More importantly, the Chalcidic League, like Macedonia, was expansionistic, which put it in direct conflict with their Macedonian neighbors.

The Macedonians had not forgotten about the war between Amyntas III and the Chalcidic League, and once Philip II had secured Macedonia's border with Thessaly, he turned his attention to enacting revenge. Philip II concentrated his efforts on Olynthus, the leading city in the Chalcidic League and a constant thorn in Macedonia's side. The war lasted until 348 BCE, when the Macedonians razed Olynthus and Philip had finally broken up the Chalcidic League for good (King, 2018, p. 83). After the victory at Olynthus, Philip II combined work and pleasure by attending the Olympic Games and hosting large, extravagant banquets. "After the capture of Olynthus, he celebrated the Olympian festival to the gods in commemoration of his victory, and offered magnificent sacrifices; and he organized a great festive assembly at which he held splendid competitions and thereafter invited many of the visiting strangers to his banquets. (Diodorus, *Library of History*, XVI, 55, 1).

Philip II's victory celebrations served important political and propaganda purposes for a number of reasons. The celebrations allowed Philip II to expand and solidify his networks with the southern Greeks, many of whom were still, no doubt, leery of the warlike Macedonian king. The celebrations also allowed Philip II to demonstrate his "Greekness," thereby establishing his rightful place among the older, more established Greek city-states.

At that point, most of the other Greeks had seen the Macedonians as Greeks, but there were still holdouts. Philip II's participation in the Olympics and his magnanimous gestures of holding extravagant *symposia* were efforts to assuage any lingering ideas the Greeks might have held regarding the Macedonians as barbarians and foreign conquerors.

The efforts were largely successful, but not all of the traditional city-states were willing to accept the Macedonians as their equals. The Athenians traditionally never saw the Macedonians as true Greeks, and although they were willing to trade with them, they were disturbed to see the Macedonians' growing influence in the Greek world. Macedonia's war against the Chalcidic League, in particular, was troubling enough for the leaders of Athens to take action. To put Philip II in his place in 349 BCE, Athens called for a renewed Hellenic League against Macedon (King, 2018, p. 83), and Philip II responded by marching the Macedonian Army south through Thessaly and central Greece until other members of the league relented by giving control of the league to the Macedonian king (King, 2018, p. 86-87).

Perhaps sensing things would get much worse if they did nothing, the Athenians declared war on Macedon in 340 BCE (King, 2018, p. 90). The first two years of the war were largely indecisive, but Philip II's army finally had favorable battlefield conditions at Chaeronea in 338 BCE. His 18 year old son, Alexander, stood with his father during the battle, taking control of the Macedonians' left flank. According to Diodorus, the battle was a complete rout. "He waited for the last of his laggard confederates to arrive, and then marched into Boeotia. His forces came to more than thirty thousand infantry and no less than two thousand cavalry…The armies deployed at dawn, and the king stationed his son Alexander, young in age but noted for his valour and swiftness of action, on one wing, placing beside him his most seasoned generals, while he himself at the head of picked men exercised the command over the other…Corpses piled up, until finally Alexander forced his way through the line and put his opponents to flight…More than a thousand Athenians fell in the battle and no less than two thousand were captured." (Diodorus, *Library of History*, XVI, 85-860).

The Battle of Chaeronea gave the Macedonians hegemony over the Greek world, and from that point on, there was very little organized or active resistance to Macedonian control of the Hellenic League due to Philip II's command of the modern and sizable Macedonian army. As mentioned above, Philip II introduced new battlefield technologies and techniques revolutionizing ancient warfare and giving Macedonians the edge over the other Greeks, and moreover, he started a practice that continued to be employed by his son, his son's successors, and even by the Romans. When Philip II brought armies onto the battlefield, they were usually comparable in size to their enemies, and constantly fielding such large armies would have been impossible with Macedonians alone, so Philip II began conscripting non-Greek soldiers from among the peoples he conquered (Hornblower, 1996, p. 905).

As Philip II won victories across Greece, questions of succession were discussed in Pella and throughout Greece. Philip II had several wives, but his son, Alexander, with his fourth wife, Olympias, seemed destined to become king (King, 2018, p. 52). Although Olympias was not Philip II's favorite queen and she was not fully Macedonian - her father was the king of Epirus - her son appeared to be the ablest of Philip's sons. The only other alternative was Arrhidaeus, who was mentally slow. The choice then seemed to be Alexander at an early point, but whether he would live that long was never a given thanks to the duplicitous nature of the Macedonian court.

After three years under the auspices of Aristotle, Alexander received his first chance to forge his own legacy when his father left Macedonia to wage war on Byzantion, leaving Alexander – aged 16 – as regent of Macedon. Philip's absence, and the presence of an untested ruler on the Macedonian throne, inspired several of Philip's subject and satellite states to revolt: the Thracians rose up in arms, but Alexander proved up to the task and crushed their forces, erecting the first of many "Alexandrias", the city of Alexandropolis in Thrace. Philip was extremely pleased with his son's performance and, in order to test his mettle further, when he returned from his campaign he dispatched Alexander, at the head of a small army, to pacify the remainder of Thrace. During this time, in 338 BC, Alexander also defeated a force sent from Illyria to attack

Macedonia, as well as succeeding in his task of quelling the revolt in Thrace. He was summoned from the field with his army by Philip, who had used a flimsy pretext to involve himself in the affairs of the Greek city-states and was marching southwards at the head of the Macedonian army. Together, they marched through the pass at Thermopylae (where, years before, a Spartan army under King Leonidas and their Thespian allies had fought one of history's most famous and legendary battles against the Persian Empire, Greece's historic enemy), defeating the Theban garrison dispatched to stop them, and advanced into Greece proper.

Once in Greece, Philip and Alexander's main concerns were the powerful cities of Thebes and Athens, which had united their armies and resources against them. They marched on the city of Amphissa, whose citizens had begun tilling fields sacred to the oracle at Delphi, prompting Philip's invasion on the pretext he had been invited by concerned followers of the oracle. After forcing Amphissa to surrender, Philip sent Thebes and Athens a last offer of peace, but upon having it rejected, marched southwards. The Macedonian army marched quickly, but it found its path blocked by the Thebans and Athenians near Chaeronea. The Thebans were confident, having recently developed an outstanding martial tradition which had led to their vanquishing none other than the renowned Spartans, and battle was rapidly joined. Philip took command of the right wing of his army and gave the left to Alexander – cannily ensuring that his most seasoned generals were there to make sure the young boy did not blunder – and Alexander did not disappoint his father's trust. As Philip lured the enemy with a false retreat, Alexander personally led a cavalry charge that smashed through the Theban forces, instigating a general rout among the Athenian troops and forcing the Thebans, alone and surrounded, to surrender. The victorious Macedonians marched southwards, where they met no further resistance and were greeted with offers of alliance by all the major cities (save Sparta, which traditionally stood aloof from such matters). Philip united these cities in what became known as the League of Corinth, an all-Greek coalition formed with the express purpose of waging war on Persia, with Philip himself as *Hegemon*, or supreme commander.

It should have been Alexander's finest hour: he had proven himself in the field, he was the hero of Chaeronea, and he enjoyed the esteem of both his father and many of the leading Macedonian nobles. However, his triumph quickly turned sour. Shortly after returning to Pella, Philip set his wife Olympias aside in favour of the young Cleopatra, the niece of one of his generals. Alexander was furious at this, particularly as it jeopardised his position as Philip's heir, and he had a violent falling-out with his father during the wedding celebrations, to the point that the ever-volatile Philip actually drew his sword on his son. Philip was well and truly drunk by then, and succeeded only in sprawling on the floor, prompting Alexander to remark, "Here is the man who you would have lead you against the Persians; he stumbles jumping from one seat to the next."

Following his quarrel with his father, Alexander was forced to flee Macedonia with Olympias, but he was recalled to court some six months after, Philip's anger having mellowed in his absence. Shortly thereafter Cleopatra gave birth to a son, also named Philip, which must have given Alexander cause for concern, and then the following year to a daughter. Yet Philip seems to have genuinely wanted to have Alexander succeed him, so much so that he wanted him by his side at a royal wedding celebration in 338 BCE. It was during these festivities that Pausanias, the captain of Philip's royal bodyguard, stabbed the king in the heart and killed him. Pausanias's motives were never established, though it his highly likely he was in Persian pay, but either way, he was killed trying to escape.

Whatever the reasons for his actions, Philip was dead, and Alexander was proclaimed king by Philip's generals and the leading men in Macedonia. At age 20, he was ruler of Macedon and *Hegemon* of the League of Corinth.

Naturally, Alexander's ascent to the throne of Macedon was not unopposed in the wake of his father's assassination. Fearful of political rivals challenging the claim of a young and relatively untested monarch whose father had died so suddenly and mysteriously, Alexander had many of his political rivals, chief among them those who had a tenable claim to the throne, executed. Olympias, who had returned from exile, also took advantage of the turmoil to have Cleopatra, Philip's widow, and her daughter by him, burned alive. It is also likely that she tried to poison Philip's son by Cleopatra, but a botched attempt (or perhaps natural causes) made him mentally disabled, and thus no longer a threat. For his part, Alexander was furious at this barbarity, which prompted an estrangement which lasted for years.

Alexander also had to contend with problems outside of Macedonia. News of the *Hegemon's* death had not gone unnoticed, and virtually all of Philip's conquests rose up in arms, as the Thracians, Thessalians, Athenians and Thebans all discarded their alliances with Macedon, rushing to occupy the passes in the north of Greece against Alexander's forces. Ignoring suggestions of a political solution to the uprising, Alexander led his cavalry on an encircling march around the Thessalian forces sent to bar his way, surrounding them and forcing them into surrender before marching southwards. The Greek city-states, terrified by the speed of his advantage, promptly sued for peace, recognizing him as *Hegemon*. Alexander was formally invested with the title in the city of Corinth, where he also famously encountered the renowned philosopher Diogenes the Cynic. Alexander, who through his tutelage by Aristotle had developed an admiration for wise men, asked Diogenes if the King of Macedon might do anything for him. Diogenes, who was sitting in the public square at the time, sourly looked up at him and told Alexander that he could; he could get out of his sun. This remark prompted Alexander to later say, "If I could not be Alexander, I would be Diogenes". Plutarch would later write that Alexander and Diogenes died on the same day in 323 BCE.

A 16th century depiction of the famous encounter between Alexander and Diogenes

His position in Greece now secure, Alexander turned northwards, and in 335 BCE he succeeded in securing his northern frontiers for good in a lightning campaign which crushed the armies of the Thracians and Illyrians utterly in a series of vicious battles. It was a remarkable display of soldiering, but one that the Greek cities seemed content to ignore: while Alexander was occupied in the Balkans, Thebes and Athens rose in revolt once more, despite their promises of friendship. Furious, Alexander marched his army southwards. This time, despite the entreaties of many of his advisors, he would show no mercy. When Thebes, abandoned by Athens, continued to resist him, he razed the city to the ground. This effectively ended all further resistance in Greece.

Instead of dedicating his time to the affairs of state, Alexander turned his attention east toward the Achaemenid Persian Empire. As soon as Xerxes I had left Greece with his army in the 5th century, the Greeks longed for revenge. The primary factor keeping the Greeks from moving forward with any plan was their disunity and propensity for infighting, but when Philip II forced his hegemony over Greece, the matter had been settled. Now, with his position as *Hegemon* firmly established, Alexander decided it was time to pursue his father's dream by invading Persia.

Unique Armies

One immensely important part of the inheritance Alexander received from his father was the deadly Macedonian army. Prior to Philip's kingship, Macedonia had been a backwater of Greece, soft and easily raided by neighboring tribes and kingdoms. They were constantly on the back foot, defending against attacks and losing valuable resources to enemy forays. Like most of Greece at that time, Macedonia did not maintain a standing army. Thus, even though the Macedonians themselves were tough and rugged and prone to fighting, they were untrained warriors in battle, and they clearly operated more like farmers and tradesmen who brought whatever tools they could find as weapons.

While a hostage in Thebes as a teenager, Philip learned the importance of training and discipline as well as flexibility and cooperative army units from the famous Theban General Epaminondas. Upon becoming king, he immediately instituted changes to Macedonian policies. He established a well-trained, well-paid standing army and tweaked their tactics. The spear-bearing phalanx had long been a Greek tradition of fighting, formed of soldiers called hoplites bearing large round shields and spears about two and a half meters in length. They were usually heavily armored as well, and in the tight phalanx formation, the shield of each soldier protected the man to his left while creating a brisling wall of spear points.

It had been a largely successful style, but Philip did not have the money to outfit his army in that fashion, so instead he modified it by dropping the armor, exchanging the hoplite spear for the *sarissa* (a spear now four to six meters in length), and giving his men slightly smaller shields. After they were drilled to perfection, this new phalanx was a formidable weapon that could break armies apart before they were even able to reach the Macedonian soldiers.

The only way to break a formation like this was to get around it to the sides or back. Traditionally the Greeks had not worried too much about being flanked, as none of them had very strong cavalry forces due to the fact their landscape was not conducive to raising horses. Any cavalry units were more like lightly armed scouts who only occasionally skirmished with other light cavalry units.

The *sarissa* phalanx was even larger and more unwieldy than the Greek hoplite phalanx, and battles at close quarters or quick changes of position were even more difficult, making the flanks that much more vulnerable. Philip solved this concern with units called *hypaspists* (lightly armed soldiers that more closely resembled the Greek hoplite), with a smaller spear, and carrying a short sword. Their job was to protect the flanks of the phalanx through their ability to turn and reposition more quickly. The training and drilling allowed the army to move so quickly from point to point that the enemy often couldn't believe that they had arrived.

Additionally, Macedonia was better suited to horses, and the Macedonians also traded with nearby Thessaly, breeders of large quality horses. Philip increased his cavalry and trained them to work in tandem with his infantry, protecting their own flanks and moving quickly around to smash the enemy's. The best cavalrymen were the sons of Greek nobles (many of them personal friends of Philip and Alexander), who functioned both as a battle unit and as a personal guard to the king. They were called the Companion Cavalry.

In contrast to Greek tactics, the Persians relied heavily on their cavalry. The open plains of Persia made excellent ground for cavalry deployment, and they had easy access to horses and camels. There were even occasionally war elephants from their provinces on the edge of India.

Persian infantry generally consisted of peasant soldiers (the more skilled foot soldiers were those fighting with ranged weapons, particularly bows and arrows) who could weaken the enemy from a distance and then support the cavalry attack. Additionally, the deployed forces were usually enormous, as Persia held a great expanse of territory from which to pull recruits.

This army had terrified the Greeks for generations, and the cavalry usually proved nearly impossible for the Greeks to handle. A common Greek tactic against the Persians was to seek a battlefield with territory difficult for horses and chariots, thereby subverting the greatest Persian asset.

At the same time, the Persian cavalry units were not the only major threats. The king's elite royal guard doubled as a standing army and consisted of 10,000 heavily armed, well-trained soldiers. It was an extremely dangerous force, as the Greeks learned at the Battle of Thermopylae during the Second Persian War.

Issus

When Alexander crossed the Hellespont in 334 BCE, his first encounter with Persian forces took place at the Battle of Granicus River. The Persian commanders had met at the city of Zeleia along with Memnon of Rhodes, the leader of their Greek mercenary forces, and Memnon advised the Persians not to fight Alexander head on. Since the Persian forces were slightly outnumbered for the battle, Memnon advised that the Persians should scorch the nearby lands and make travel and supplying the army difficult for Alexander.

Ultimately, however, the Persians did not trust the Greek commander and were unwilling to destroy their own lands. It's quite likely they thought that the young inexperienced king at the head of a Greek army would not be too difficult to defeat. Instead, they decided to draw Alexander into a defensive position of their own choosing.

Against a lesser general, their strategy might have worked well. They lined up on the far side of the Granicus, a fairly wide river with a steep bank to climb, and upon seeing the disadvantage, Parmenion advised Alexander to wait until nightfall and cross upstream. When Alexander refused Parmenion's advice and made an attack at once, he startled the Persians. He led the charge himself on the right wing of the line, cleverly advancing in an oblique line in order to counteract the current and emerge with a flat, strong line on the other side of the river.

LA VERIV SVRMONTE TOVT OBSTACLE.

VIRTVS OMNI OBICE MAIOR.

A painting of the Macedonians crossing the river by Charles Le Brun

A statue of Parmenion

The first Macedonians to successfully cross in the middle took heavy casualties in the unsure footing of the river and the climb to reach the enemy, but before too long, Alexander's cavalry had made the crossing and smashed into the Persian left wing. As more and more Macedonians made it to the other side and engaged the Persian forces, the crossing became easier for those behind, so soon the majority of the army had arrived.

With the strength of the Macedonian army on the enemy bank, the advantage turned toward Alexander. The numbers were fairly even, with both armies having between 30,000 and 40,000 men, but there were crucial advantages for the Macedonians. Alexander's soldiers were fighting with heavy wooden spears against light Persian lances, and the Macedonian standing army already had several years of experience in campaigning. While the Greek mercenaries fighting for the Persians had combat experience, many of the Persians were raw recruits called up from local villages to mount a defense.

The fighting was fierce, and as more Macedonians made their way across the river to join the battle, the Persian center began to crumble and then collapsed. That was followed by the collapse of the army's wings, leading to a complete rout.

About 1,000 Persians were killed, but Alexander did not pursue the fleeing soldiers. Instead, he turned to deal with the Greek mercenaries, who were still standing in battle formation. The ancient writer Arrian claimed that this was not due to some extraordinary demonstration of courage, but rather because they were shocked by the abrupt change of fortune. Surrounded on all sides, 2,000 were captured and the rest were massacred.

A painting of the battle by Charles Le Brun

After the Battle of the Granicus, Alexander moved south through Asia Minor, encountering occasional resistance and sieges at various cities, but he did not meet the Persians in a direct battle again until Issus. Disappointed by the failure at Granicus and concerned by Alexander's ongoing success, Darius III resolved to lead the battle himself in the next engagement. He had not been king for very long, but the Persians had not lost a battle that he had personally led.

A depiction of Darius III in the Alexander Mosaic found in Pompeii

Darius III gathered a massive force, probably somewhere around 100,000 soldiers, and set out from Babylon to intercept Alexander. He camped on a large open plain, an advantageous position for his cavalry, and hoped that Alexander would come to him. However, as the days passed, Darius grew impatient and began to believe, along with his advisors, that Alexander feared to face him.

In reality, Alexander had been detained by his own impetuousness. On a hot summer day, he decided that the Cydnus looked ideal for a swim, but the frigid water sent his body into a mild shock, and he soon became seriously ill to the point of unconsciousness. The Macedonians were horribly worried, but finally Alexander slowly began to regain consciousness and recognize his friends grouped anxiously around his bedside.

By the time Alexander had recovered enough to march out, Darius had already begun to fret and move northward, seeking his foe. He actually passed Alexander's forces in his march to the north, for Parmenion had taken the town of Issus, and Alexander marched south to join him there. Parmenion advised that the narrow pass a small distance from the town provided an excellent tactical location to face the larger Persian force, and Alexander agreed, so they moved the army to encamp there.

Issus was left unguarded, and some wounded Macedonians were left there who were unfit for the coming battle. Sadly, they fell victim to a power play by the Persians, though it may well have been a disadvantage in the end, because the fates that befell them spurred the Macedonians on. Coming unexpectedly from the north, Darius retook Issus, and though normally a kind king, Darius was urged by his advisors to make an example of the wounded men. Some of them were tortured and killed, but a few had their hands cut off and cauterized. After that, they were marched around so that they could see the immense strength of the Persian army before being sent back to their own army to report to Alexander the size of the force that faced him.

Alexander positioned his soldiers in the narrow pass just as he had hoped to, completely neutralizing the cavalry advantage of the Persians and lowering the number of soldiers that could directly face his men. With his flanks anchored and protected by the sea inlet on their left and the hills on the right, Darius still hoped to decide the battle with his cavalry and to avoid the deadly Macedonian phalanx. He positioned his heavy mounted soldiers opposite Alexander's Thessalian cavalry along the side of the water inlet, the area most conducive to cavalry movements, and kicked off the battle by sending them charging against the Greeks. The Thessalian cavalry struggled, but with a series of charges and regrouping together, they held their position against the onslaught. In the center, Alexander's phalanx had to make it through the river and climb a bank (like at Granicus), so they suffered heavy losses against Darius's Greek mercenaries.

Alexander himself began the battle with his companion cavalry, alongside the *hypaspists* on the right flank, who managed to punch a hole in the Persian infantry in heavy hand-to-hand fighting and collapse the Persian left wing. Alexander led a furious charge directly towards Darius III, who tried to remain calm and command his soldiers in the face of the onslaught. However, soon he was surrounded by the bodies of "his most famous generals who had succumbed to a glorious death before the eyes of their king, and who now all lay face-down where they had fallen fighting."[1] Even the horses drawing his chariot suffered wounds and began to panic, and finally Darius could not hold out any longer. Rather than being taken or killed, he mounted a horse behind his chariot, left his royal insignia, and rode from the field.

When they saw their king flee, the Persian army broke and fled with him, pursued by the Macedonians until dark. It was a costly loss for Persia. Morale was shattered given that they had lost to an inferior force with their own king leading the fight. The number of Persians killed was also horrifyingly high, particularly in the slaughter of the route. Alexander's general and companion Ptolemy reported that when the group pursuing Darius came to a ravine, they were able to cross it easily by simply walking across the bodies of the dead that filled it.

---

[1] Curtius, 3.11.7–12.

An ancient bust of Ptolemy

Darius's mother, wife, daughters, and son were captured along with the baggage train, but Alexander treated them with great respect. In fact, he and Darius's mother, Sisygambis, grew so fond of one another that he continued to call her "mother" for the remainder of his life. She in turn was so disappointed at Darius's abandonment and so appreciative of Alexander's kindness that she remained devoted to him and never fully forgave her own son's actions.[2]

---

[2] Arrian, 2.11.6–12.5; Diodorus, 2.17.37.

The Alexander Mosaic's depiction of the Battle of Issus

The Battle of Issus by Jan Brueghel the Elder

Moving to Gaugamela

After the victory at Issus, Alexander decided not to pursue Darius into the interior of Persian territory, but to continue his efforts to secure the coastline. He continued south, capturing cities in a number of spectacular sieges, until eventually most would surrender to him upon his approach.

Meanwhile, Darius reformed and regrouped, raising a second large army for the next engagement with Alexander, even as the Macedonians drove the Persian occupying forces out of Egypt and were welcomed as liberators by the Egyptians. Alexander was careful to show deep respect for the Egyptian gods and customs, and as a result, he was honored and named pharaoh of Egypt.

The Macedonian army wintered in the Nile Valley, enjoying relaxation in the warm sun of Egypt and the eager friendliness of the Egyptians. Alexander himself, with several of his closest friends, traveled extensively throughout Egypt, visiting the oracle at the Oasis of Siwa, where he was reportedly declared to be the son of Zeus-Ammon and therefore divine. How much Alexander actually believed in his own divinity is largely speculative, but several comments made to his close friends, along with a long speech praising his own father, Philip II, later on in his campaigns suggest that his embrace of his godly father was probably mostly for the benefit of his subjects, a propaganda point to instill awe and devotion and improve morale. During his travels in Egypt, he also established the city of Alexandria, which would grow to become the most important trade emporium in the Mediterranean. Of course, Alexander never had the chance to see his vision become reality at Alexandria.

Reuniting with his army, Alexander finally led them out of Egypt in the late spring of 331 BCE, prepared to again engage with Darius and finally defeat the Persian Empire. They marched across the Sinai Peninsula and back to the city of Tyre, where they met the fleet and rested for a short time. Alexander hosted a great festival of Greek games and arts in honor of Heracles, attracting the foremost athletes and actors of the day. He also received a number of embassies from foreign lands offering treaties and asking for assistance.

During this time, a detachment was sent ahead to the Euphrates River with instructions to bridge it, but they could not complete the task as Darius had also sent his own commander, Mazaeus, with a small group of soldiers to defend the crossing. When Alexander's army arrived around July or early August 331 BCE, Mazaeus immediately withdrew, but Alexander lost further time as he now had to wait for the construction of the bridges to be completed.

Every event that delayed Alexander's advance was to the Persians' advantage. Darius, though not an adaptable military genius like Alexander, was no fool. He possessed the entire infrastructure of the Persian Empire and the ability to maintain strong internal supply lines while Alexander and his men moved in unfamiliar territory, supported only by recently conquered territory. He also knew that his own royal person was the key to the Persian Empire. To complete his conquest, Alexander needed to capture or kill Darius, which meant Alexander would at some point have to come to him. Any delays merely worked in Darius's favor, offering him more time to gather resources and muster a new army from his many vassal states, as he had been doing during Alexander's sojourn in Egypt. It also gave him more time to prepare his army, drilling them in battle maneuvers and improving the communication between soldiers and units from a large variety of cultures and languages. He learned the lessons taught by his failure at Issus and sought to rectify them in the coming battle.

Alexander, meanwhile, took his time on the march down Mesopotamia, choosing a longer route which provided better food supplies for the army and their animals. Although he had received reports that Darius had gathered another army, he expected it to be small, weak, and ineffectual, believing that the main brunt of Darius's forces had been shattered at Issus. In fact, when the Macedonians captured some of Darius's scouts and they informed him that Darius had gathered yet another massive army, he initially discounted the tales.

As Alexander's army continued the march through Mesopotamia and crossed the Tigris River heading towards Assyria, Darius was busy choosing the best possible ground for the coming battle. At Issus, the geographical features of the battlefield had played to Alexander's advantage, allowing the young Macedonian to anchor the two sides of his army against steep slopes and minimize the threat from Darius's vast forces by limiting the number of soldiers that could come into contact with the Macedonian line at any given time. The Persian king had made the mistake of pursuing Alexander, even at the loss of his highly strategic position, and this time, he would not commit the same error again.

Darius made camp on the vast Plains of Gaugamela, a short distance from the larger city of Arbela, with no intention of moving. Alexander would have to come to him, and he was content to wait, improving his army with every day that passed. On such an open field, Alexander would have no solid protection for his exposed flanks, and the vast numbers of the Persian forces could theoretically envelop the Greeks without ever significantly thinning the Persian line.

Like at Issus, Darius's plan relied heavily on his use of the superior Persian cavalry. He had a large number of infantry, but they were insignificant when matched against the Greeks. As mentioned before, Persia had long relied upon their cavalry, and with the exception of the 10,000 elite Immortals, bodyguards of the king, their infantry consisted largely of bowmen and slingers. Even the Immortals with their standard-length spears were hardly a match for the Macedonian *sarissa* phalanx. Moreover, most of Darius's infantry were new, raw recruits who would be facing experienced soldiers who had grown up in the far more hostile lands of Macedonia and had been campaigning for years, if not decades.

All of this was obvious to the Persian leader, who considered his infantry to be nothing more than a reserve. In fact, he hoped to not have to use them in the battle at all, so they were arrayed behind Darius and the Immortals, with the full line of cavalry in front.

It was on this cavalry that Darius pinned his hopes for victory. The Persian cavalry was a formidable force, and it had been bolstered by the arrival of Bessus, satrap of Bactria, with the renowned Bactrian and Scythian cavalry units. Darius intended to execute a double flanking maneuver, sending his fast cavalry units around both sides of Alexander's army to crash into the phalanxes from the sides and rear, while in the center of the line, he would rely on his surprise shock troops, the scythed chariots, to smash through and break the elite Macedonian phalanx. According to Arrian, Darius also had 15 war elephants for the center of the line, which was hardly an immense number that could carry the day, but might serve to terrify the Macedonians and their horses. It's likely none of them had previously seen an elephant, and certainly not one charging at their lines.

Other sources do not mention the war elephants, and it is unclear whether Arrian confused Gaugamela and the later Battle of Hydaspes in this regard. However, Arrian's main source was one of Alexander's foremost generals, Ptolemy, who was most certainly present at the heat of the battle and likely rode with Alexander's Companion Cavalry. If the information came from Ptolemy, it is unlikely he would have confused those two events, though it is still potentially an error on the part of Arrian or another of his sources.

With so much hope riding on his cavalry, Darius spared no pains to ensure their success. Gaugamela was the perfect ground for a massive cavalry assault, with plenty of room for the Persians to envelop the smaller Greek line. He even improved the field of battle, for after camping there with his army, he set his soldiers to work leveling the ground, filling holes, and removing any large rocks that could interfere with the movement of the horses. With his battleground set, Darius could only wait for the eventual arrival of Alexander and his army.

While journeying south into Mesopotamia, disaster struck Alexander's baggage train. One of the captured Persian eunuchs begged an audience with Alexander to inform him that Darius's wife was seriously ill and barely breathing. Before the Macedonian king could respond, a second messenger arrived to inform them that she had died. As ancient writer Quintus Curtius Rufus put it, "One would have thought that Alexander's tears were being shed among his own relatives and that he was in need of receiving consolation rather than giving it. He took no food, and accorded every honour to the funeral ceremony, which was celebrated in traditional Persian fashion, thus showing himself truly worthy of the great reputation which he still enjoys for clemency and self-discipline. He had seen the queen only once, on the day of her capture, when he had gone to see not her but Darius' mother, and her outstanding beauty had inspired in him not lust but behaviour redounding to his glory."[3]

In the general commotion of the queen's death, another of the captive eunuchs, Tyriotes, slipped out of an unguarded gate and hurried to Darius's camp. He came before Darius in deep mourning, weeping and tearing his clothes, and Darius feared that Tyriotes had come to tell him

---

[3] Curtius, 10.18–24.

that his family had been tortured and violated. Tyriotes assured him that Alexander had given the entire family the utmost respect, but he informed the Persian king that his wife was dead. Darius could not believe that she had died unmolested, and in grief and anger, he cried, "Alexander, what is the great crime I have committed against you? Which of your relations did I kill that my cruelty should merit such punishment? Your hatred of me is unprovoked, but even supposing the war you have started is just, should you have fought it with women?" At this, Tyriotes again swore that Alexander and his men had not committed any violence against her, insisting that Alexander had grieved as sincerely as Darius himself. It was the wrong assertion, for Darius's suspicions grew even greater, as he was certain that Alexander would only weep like that for a lost lover. When he threatened to torture Tyriotes for the truth, Tyriotes still refused to budge, and he "offered to undergo torture, calling the gods to witness that the queen had been treated with propriety and respect. Finally, accepting the truth of the eunuch's words, Darius covered his head and wept for a long time. Then, with tears still streaming from his eyes, he uncovered his face and held his hands up to the sky. 'Gods of my country,' he said, 'before all else make firm my rule; but my next prayer, if my career is at an end, is that Asia find no other ruler than this just enemy, this merciful victor.'"[4]

In response to Alexander's clemency, Darius attempted one final time to make peace through diplomacy and gain the Macedonian as an ally. He sent envoys to Alexander to let him know that Darius was sending the offer primarily in gratefulness for the treatment of his family. Due to his kindness, Darius knew Alexander to be an honorable man, so he offered Alexander all of the territory west of the Euphrates River, 30,000 talents of silver, and the hand of one of his daughters in marriage. This would place Alexander in the position of his son and ensure he shared the rule of Persia with Darius.

Alexander brought all of his top generals and advisors to council and asked them to freely speak their minds. Only Parmenion had the courage to voice what most of them were thinking, saying, "If I were Alexander, I should accept what was offered and make a treaty." Alexander, it is said, simply smiled and replied, "And so I would if I were Parmenion. But I am Alexander, so I cannot."[5]

To the envoys, Alexander responded that they had obviously forgotten from where they were speaking to them. He was already on the eastern side of the Euphrates and had already taken the land that Darius offered him. Additionally, he held the daughter that Darius offered him and had no desire to be Darius's son-in-law. Rather, he offered that if Darius sought a life of leisure, he should submit himself to Alexander's rule and rule only those under him, giving Alexander supreme power. Otherwise, he must prepare himself to determine the boundaries of their respective empires through battle.

The ambassadors thanked Alexander that he had not attempted to deceive them with false

---

[4] Curtius 10.25–34.
[5] Diodorus, 2.6.53.

hopes of peaceful negotiations and returned immediately to Darius to inform him that a final battle was now imminent.[6]

The Battle of Gaugamela

Alexander and his army advanced toward the Persians and the plains of Gaugamela, stopping on a small hill a short distance away. Alexander ordered his men to build a palisade and fortify the hill, intending to leave the larger portion of the baggage train and any injured soldiers safely out of the battle. As they labored at this task, the mists of morning slowly cleared, revealing the plain below, flooded with the massive Persian force. The Macedonians let out a battle cry, and the returning shout from the Persians was deafening. Alexander was now faced outright with just how strong of a force Darius had gathered, something he had not previously believed.

In a council with his generals, Parmenion once again spoke out and advised a night attack, saying that in the confusion of a surprise attack, the enemy could be crushed. He was loudly supported by Polyperchon. Loathe to chastise Parmenion again so soon, Alexander instead responded to Polyperchon: "'The subterfuge you recommend to me is characteristic of brigands and thieves,' he said, 'for deception is their only aim. But I shall not permit Darius' absence, narrow terrain or a furtive attack at night to detract from my glory. My decision is to attack in broad daylight. I prefer to live to regret my bad luck than to be ashamed of my victory.'"[7]

Darius had considered the same limitations of Alexander's numbers, and he too thought that the Macedonian king would choose to attack by night. He had therefore ordered the majority of his army to stand in formation, ready for battle, throughout the night. It was certainly a reasonable assumption, but Darius had not counted on Alexander's high regard for honor, nor on a number of other perfectly sound military reasons to avoid a night engagement. The dark could be treacherous, and a loss at night would likely not push Darius to concede defeat, as he would assume that it was just an accident of the poor battle conditions. Additionally, if anything went wrong, the Macedonians were in unfriendly and unfamiliar territory surrounded by enemies. Without a decisive victory, they would be left in dire straits in the dark of night, with no idea where to go or who to turn to.[8]

Though Darius had every reason to expect a night attack, the decision was still a grave detriment to him. His men stayed awake in formation throughout the night while Alexander's army slept soundly, putting the fatigued Persians at a disadvantage from the beginning. When the morning sun began to rise, they would grow hot and dehydrated as well. On top of that, "fear naturally generated by the prospect of danger, did not come in one immediate and automatic rush, but occupied their thoughts over a long period until it dominated their minds."[9]

---

[6] Curtius, 11.14–23.
[7] Curtius, 13.7–9.
[8] Arrian, 3.10.2–4.
[9] Arrian, 3.11.2.

Alexander was also consumed by concern for the following day. He had seen the entire array of the Persian forces, including their large cavalry, their vicious scythed chariots, and several elephants. However, in the early hours of the following morning, he had finally outlined his plan for the battle the next day, and confident that he had struck upon the best possible strategy, he fell into a deep sleep: "At daybreak, after assembling to receive their orders, the officers were amazed at the silence surrounding the king's tent. Usually Alexander would send for them, and sometimes there were sharp words for the dawdlers. Now they were astonished that at this crucial juncture he had failed to wake up, and they believed that he was not sleeping but shrinking with fear. None of his bodyguards dared enter the tent, however, even though the moment of decision was at hand, and the men could neither take up arms nor proceed to their ranks without Alexander's command. After a long delay Parmenion took it upon himself to tell the men to eat, and only when it was imperative for them to move out of camp did he finally enter Alexander's tent. After calling him by name several times, he woke him with his hand since he could not with his voice. 'It's broad daylight,' he said. 'The enemy have brought up their army in battle-formation, while your men are still not under arms, waiting for your command. What has happened to your old alertness? Usually you are waking up the watch!' Alexander replied, 'Do you think I could have fallen asleep before easing my mind of the worries that kept me from resting?' Then he ordered the trumpet-signal to be given for battle. And when Parmenion kept on expressing surprise at the king's claim to have enjoyed a carefree sleep, 'It's not a bit surprising,' he said. 'When Darius was burning the land, destroying villages and ruining our food supplies, I was beside myself with despair. But now that he is preparing to decide the issue in battle, what do I have to fear? Good heavens, he has answered my prayers!'"[10]

The Persians were arrayed with their strongest shock units, the scythed chariots and the elephants, front and center in their line. Behind them Darius stood in his chariot, surrounded by his mounted and unmounted bodyguards, the royal horse guards, and the 10,000 Immortals, who were in turn flanked by Greek mercenaries. Mazaeus commanded cavalry units from Syria and Mesopotamia on the right flank, while Bessus led the elite Bactrian and Scythian cavalry on the left flank. Behind them all were the less effective Persian infantry units in support. Ancient authors estimate Darius's forces numbered anywhere from 250,000-1,000,000. Modern estimates tend to be much lower but still think the Persians had between 100,000 and 250,000 soldiers and outnumbered the Macedonians by at least two to one.[11]

---

[10] Curtius, 13.17–25.
[11] Everitt, 204–205.

THE BATTLE OF ARBELA

A 1913 engraving depicting a scene from the battle

Alexander, knowing that he had to somehow counter the Persian attempts to outflank his outnumbered force, lined up his men in an oblique line rather than a straight line. This would mean that any enemy force wishing to envelop them would have to travel significantly further to complete the outflanking maneuver, thereby drawing and thinning the Persian line. Alexander's left flank, drawing back from the enemy in a diagonal, was commanded by Parmenion, while the far extreme of the flank was anchored by the tough Thessalian cavalry. The middle of the left leg of the army held the elite Macedonian phalanx, armed with their *sarissas*. To the right of them were the silver shields, a unit more equipped for hand-to-hand fighting, with the archers, javelin throwers, and other ranged units ahead of them.

The right side of the army also drew back diagonally from the tip, though far less distant, and it held cavalry backed by mercenary infantry. Like the silver shields, these men would not have held the giant *sarissa* favored by the unbreakable phalanx but instead carried smaller shields or short swords for close combat. Behind all of his men, Alexander had arrayed a rear, support phalanx of his *sarissa*-men, near a small amount of baggage, with orders to be prepared to turn and face the enemy if they managed to get around the main bulk of the army. The total force was around 30,000–50,000 men. At the center point of the triangle he had created, Alexander led his Companion Cavalry, the elite bodyguard unit comprised mainly of the sons of nobles and Alexander's childhood friends.[12]

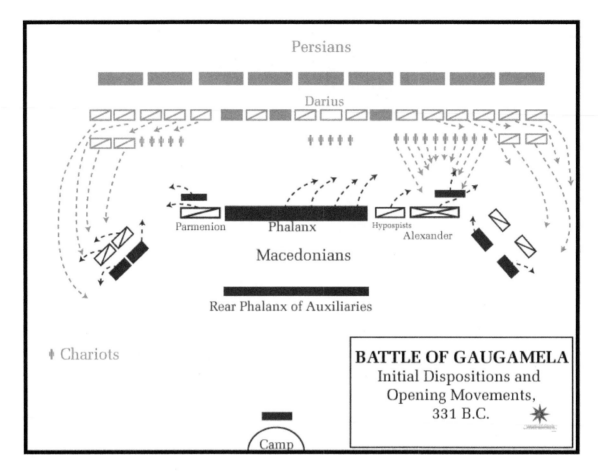

Persians

Darius

Parmenion   Phalanx   Hypospists   Alexander

Macedonians

Rear Phalanx of Auxiliaries

Chariots

BATTLE OF GAUGAMELA
Initial Dispositions and
Opening Movements,
331 B.C.

Camp

A map of the lines

The morale of Alexander's soldiers played a huge role in enabling them to face such a massive force. Alexander had emerged from his tent in excellent spirits, and the men were heavily bolstered by his confidence. As they drew up their lines for battle, Alexander mounted one of his horses and rode down the length of his army, calling out personal greetings, recalling their shared exploits, and giving exhortations to the soldiers along the way. Though certainly an excellent tactician and general, a key component to Alexander's success was his intimate charisma. Just before beginning the battle, he switched horses and mounted Bucephalus, the giant black stallion who had been his horse since he was a teenager. Bucephalus was now older, so Alexander spared him the effort of the battle preparations, but he would still ride no other horse into battle.[13]

Fighting began on the right flank, which was closer to the enemy. As the two armies advanced toward one another, Alexander led his right wing further and further to the right, while the archers and javelin throwers filled the gap left behind. Bessus's cavalry rode parallel, following Alexander's movement, until Darius began to worry that Alexander would draw the battle away from the area that his men had so carefully leveled for battle. He therefore ordered his cavalry to

[12] Ibid.
[13] Worthington, 190.

engage. Alexander sent in his mercenary cavalry to engage, and though they were pushed back, he continued to deploy reinforcements to keep Bessus's forces busy on the flank.[14]

In a brilliant move, Alexander kept his infantry units behind his cavalry, and when they burst out and surprised the Persian cavalry, it was a demoralizing shock. The Macedonians managed to push back the Persians, compelling Bessus to commit even more of his men and removing them entirely from the rest of the field.

While Alexander had not quite achieved the outcome he desired, he had greatly minimized Darius's strength and the number of enemy forces that could be sent against his main line. The cavalry on Darius's right wing were also stretched out and busy, having had to travel far around Alexander's oblique left wing in an attempt to outflank them.

With his cavalry busy, Darius turned to his elephants and scythed chariots, sending them charging against the Macedonian phalanx.[15] The veteran Macedonians, showing extreme fortitude, stood up to the oncoming charge. The archers and javelin men did their best to eliminate the drivers before they reached the line, and pursuant to Alexander's orders, when the Persians got near the phalanx, the soldiers began to bang their spears against their shields, attempting to spook the charging animals. A large number did indeed veer off, and as the remainder came upon the phalanx, Alexander's deeply disciplined troops sidestepped as a unit with split second timing to open lanes in their lines, allowing the chariots to harmlessly pass. Now surrounded by the enemy with the ranged units at their backs, the animals and drivers became easy targets for spear throwers, who wrapped back around to continue the attack. In some instances, the Macedonians were able to merely run forward and grab the reins of the horses, bringing them under control. Those that made it past the main line were captured by the rearguard.

The chariots were still a lethal weapon, however, and they were not completely countered without any damage being done: "Such was the keenness and the force of the scythes ingeniously contrived to do harm that they severed the arms of many, shields and all, and in no small number of cases they cut through necks and sent heads tumbling to the ground with the eyes still open and the expression of the countenance unchanged, and in other cases they sliced through ribs with mortal gashes and inflicted a quick death…The ground was littered with the severed limbs of soldiers and, as there was no pain while the wounds were still warm, the men did not in fact drop their weapons, despite the mutilation and their weakness, until they dropped dead from loss of blood."[16] Still, they had failed to break and terrify the Macedonian army as Darius had hoped. The line remained intact, and it continued to advance toward the Persians. Darius's secret weapon and most important strategic unit had largely failed.[17]

---

[14] Worthington, 191.
[15] Everitt, 207
[16] Curtius, 15.17
[17] Diodorus, 2.6.58.

By this time, the dust was so thick from the movements of men and horses that each commander was fighting almost in isolation, but this was in Alexander's favor. Distracted and losing sight of the remainder of the Persian army, Bessus finally threw too many of his cavalry too far to the left and opened a gap in the Persian army, which was exactly what Alexander had hoped. Spotting the opening, "he wheeled for the gap, formed a wedge of the Companion cavalry and the immediately adjacent infantry section, and led them on at full speed and in full cry straight for Darius."[18]

On the Macedonian right flank, Parmenion's forces were enduring a fierce onslaught by Mazaeus and his cavalry, but still holding their own. For all his dismissal of Parmenion in the days leading up to the battle, Parmenion was still Alexander's best general and tactician. He had fought under Philip for years, with Philip having once said of him that he had many great nobles, but only one true general. There was a reason why Alexander trusted him with the large left flank.

Parmenion's job was essentially to bear the brunt of the attack and hold fast long enough for Alexander to make his move on Darius. Though the Macedonians held up, they were hard pressed, to the point that Mazaeus felt confident enough in his numbers that he sent a detachment of 3,000 cavalrymen around the edge of the Macedonian left flank to raid their baggage train back on the fortified hill.[19] The ancient writer Diodorus described the scene: "As they burst into the camp of the Macedonians, some of the captives seized weapons and aided the Scythians in seizing the baggage. There was shouting and confusion throughout the whole camp area at this unexpected event. Most of the female captives rushed off to welcome the Persians, but the mother of Dareius, Sisygambis, did not heed when the women called upon her, but remained placidly where she was, since she neither trusted the uncertain turns of Fortune nor would sully her gratitude toward Alexander."[20]

In the center of the line, the situation had become precarious as well. The *hypaspists* had moved into the opening left by Alexander's charge on the right. The phalanx had also begun to split in the chaos of the action, with half moving toward the gap made by the *hypaspists* and the other half inching left in response to Mazaeus's pressure on Parmenion's forces. The movement left a hole, and a group of Persian cavalry burst through it, probably initially planning to wrap around and attack Parmenion's wing from behind, a move that would have been disastrous for the tightly formed phalanx. However, as was common in cavalry charges, the horsemen grew ecstatic on the strength of the charge and overshot their target, careening through the reserve line and then beginning to attack those guarding the small amount of baggage sitting behind the Macedonian army, eagerly hoping for the right to loot what was there.

A vicious scuffle began, and the unprepared baggage guards were heavily harassed.

---

[18] Arrian, 3.14.2.

[19]

[20] Diodorus, 2.6.59.

Additionally, some Persian prisoners held there broke loose and joined the fight. However, Alexander's rear phalanx was positioned for exactly such an event. They wheeled around and reformed their line, and then made a deadly attack on the small contingent of Persian cavalry. "The commanders of the reserve line behind the front phalanx quickly gathered what was happening, turned their division about face, as were their standing orders, and came up at the Persians' rear. Many of the Persians were killed where they were caught crowded among the baggage-animals, but some broke away and escaped."[21] With the threat from the rear now neutralized, the gap was able to close up and the reserve phalanx turned their formation once again to support the rest of the army.

Back on the right, Alexander's thundering charge plowed through the horse guards and the Greek mercenaries and engaged in fierce hand-to-hand combat with the king's Immortals, always pushing towards Darius. "The cavalry with Alexander and Alexander himself brought concerted pressure to bear, shoving with their horses and stabbing their lances at the Persians' faces, followed soon by the onslaught of a solid Macedonian phalanx bristling with pikes."[22] Alexander was fully aware that Darius was the key to victory, and that if he could capture or kill the king, the war would be over. He fought wildly to reach Darius, even throwing a spear that killed Darius's chariot driver, but Darius also understood the risks. With Alexander drawing nearer and his chariot blocked in by bodies and teeming soldiers, he slipped off the back onto a nearby horse and abandoned the battlefield.

Darius has been heavily criticized by historians as a coward, but this is an incomplete picture of the situation based on the viewpoint of the Greek and Macedonian historians who came from a vastly different culture. Much of Greece, with the exception of Sparta, which did not send soldiers to accompany Alexander's campaign, had discarded their monarchies and followed democratic systems. Even the Macedonians, who maintained a king, had a very different approach to their ruler than the Persians. The king maintained a low distance power structure, meaning he did not hold airs and place himself far above his men. Even after Alexander began making claims to be the son of Zeus-Ammon, he still dressed little different from his noblemen, and his friends addressed him by his first name. Sisygambis, Darius's mother, even mistook Hephaestion for Alexander upon their first introduction, as there was nothing to distinguish Alexander as the king. Furthermore, there are indications that the Macedonian kingship was not exclusively an inherited position, but had to be either chosen or affirmed by the Macedonian nobles. If Alexander had fallen in battle, one of his highest-ranking generals could conceivably have stepped in and at least hold the army together until further decisions could be made.

By contrast, the Persian culture was one of very high distance to the power structure and an absolute ruler. Darius was believed to be divinely chosen and far superior to his subjects, and the trappings of the kingship were meant to reinforce that. It was something accepted as normal by

---

[21] Arrian, 3.14.6.
[22] Arrian, 3.14.3

Persian society. Darius had absolute final say, and his children were expected to inherit the throne. Unfortunately for him, at that time, he had no heir, as he had two older daughters who could not inherit. He may have had a son, but if so, his son was only a boy and was already Alexander's prisoner. Thus, if Darius was captured or killed, it would spell the end of the world's greatest empire.

Darius's flight may have been in part motivated by fear, but it was also a necessary, calculated action for the preservation of Persia. Alive and free, he could continue the fight. From a Persian point of view, there would be no tragic honor in his fighting to the end the way there would have been for the Greeks.

Although Darius's choice was logically sound, it certainly did nothing for the morale of his men on the battlefield. Seeing their king ride away, the infantrymen, inexperienced and afraid, immediately broke and ran. They had not even fought in the battle, and now they had no interest in doing so. Seeing the growing rout, Bessus made the order to his cavalrymen to retreat from the Persian left, deciding to leave in an orderly fashion rather than have his soldiers end up scattered and lost, unprepared for a future engagement.

At this point in the battle, the ancient writers claim that Alexander took up the pursuit of Darius, though the huge cloud of dust kicked up by the enemy made it impossible to accurately follow the Persian king in his flight. When Alexander had traveled some distance from the battlefield, he was overtaken by a messenger from Parmenion informing him that his forces were pressed and desperately needed reinforcements to win the day. Though frustrated to lose Darius, Alexander abandoned the chase and turned around to return to Parmenion.[23]

Some ancient historians have accused Parmenion of performing poorly, that he had been timid and indecisive in the battle, and that his plea for help was an unnecessary one that delayed the conquest of Persia, but this can hardly be reconciled with the events of the battle itself. Parmenion had been given the command of the crucial left wing for a reason, and furthermore, the positioning of Alexander's army and his plan to create a gap in the Persian line through which he could directly attack Darius indicate that Parmenion's role was a defensive one. He was intended to take the brunt of the attack and to hold as long as possible against the heaviest onslaught, giving Alexander time to get to Darius.[24]

Anthony Everitt came up with an intriguing idea about the nature of the message from Parmenion. He argued, not without merit, that Alexander was far too experienced a general to abandon the battlefield before being sure of the final outcome, so Everitt believed that the communication from Parmenion was not a plea for assistance, but rather a message intending to give Alexander information that could be crucial to his decision to launch his decisive charge. The fact that the message did not arrive until after the charge was due to the messenger being

---

[23] Chugg, 5.86.
[24] Plutarch, 33.9.

unable to locate Alexander in the chaos and dust before the crucial moment when Alexander had to make his move.[25]

Regardless of the intent behind the communication, Alexander knew that an ongoing pursuit of Darius was both dangerous and largely pointless. Darius could turn from the direct path from Gaugamela at any time and Alexander would be powerless to see it in the dust, and what good would his victory do if a large portion of his experienced army was slaughtered. He therefore turned back toward his line, heading for the far right of the Persian wing in order to charge them from behind and hopefully encourage a rout.

By this point, however, Mazaeus and his cavalry had caught wind of what had taken place. Their attack slackened, and their forces began to break and run. Quintus Curtius Rufus explained, "Although ignorant of why the attack had lost its impetus, Parmenion quickly seized the chance of victory. He had the Thessalian cavalry summoned to him and said: 'Do you see how after making a furious attack on us a moment ago those men are retreating in sudden panic? It must be that our king's good fortune has brought victory for us too. The battlefield is completely covered with Persian dead. What are you waiting for? Aren't you a match even for soldiers in flight?' His words rang true, and fresh hope revived their drooping spirits. At a gallop they charged their enemy, who started to give ground not just gradually but swiftly."

The fleeing cavalry ran headlong into Alexander's cavalry riding in, and there, at the latest stage of the battle, began the absolute fiercest of the fighting. The Persians managed to reform their line to some extent, and in formation they threw themselves upon Alexander's Companion Cavalry. They were no longer fighting in the hope for unscathed victory, but desperately fighting for survival. Arrian wrote, "They had no use now for the usual cavalry tactics — no throwing of javelins, no maneuvering of horses — but it was each man for himself, trying to force his own way through as the only means of survival: they were not fighting now for someone else's victory, but for their very own lives, trading blows with reckless abandon."[26] Alexander lost 60 of his Companion Cavalry in this one engagement. Hephaestion, Alexander's dearest friend, took a heavy spear wound in the arm, and three other commanders (Perdiccas, Coenus, and Menidas) were dangerously wounded by arrows.

Those that broke through Alexander's contingent continued their wild flight from the battlefield, and by this time, the entire Persian army was in a rout. Alexander and his soldiers pursued the fleeing enemy, with the cavalry catching those on foot and slaughtering as many as they could. Andrew Chugg vividly described what happened: "Some fled by the shortest available route out of there, whilst others made for remote woodlands and tracks of which their pursuers were unaware. Cavalry and infantry were intermingled and unled; the armed were mixed up with the disarmed and the unscathed marched amongst many that bled. From then on compassion was consumed by dread and amidst mutual lamentation those that could not keep up

---

[25] Everitt, 210.
[26] Arrian, 3.15.4.

were left for dead. The fleeing Persians were parched by thirst, particularly the injured and the spent, so that they sprawled facedown scattered along all the streams with mouths immersed as onwards the waters went. Since, when the water became muddy, they still gulped it avidly, the pressure of the slime distended their bellies quite promptly, such that their legs became sluggish and slack. Being then overtaken by the enemy, they were goaded by renewed attack, so that the whole region became bedecked with bodies by the butchery. Some, finding the nearby brooks occupied, turned further aside, to glean whatever hidden moisture trickled anywhere. Thus there was no pool so drained or so secluded that its thirsty trackers were eluded. And indeed from the villages closest to the road there resounded the wailing of women and the pleas of old men, calling in the barbarian fashion upon Darius, their sovereign up until then."[27]

Estimates of Persian losses range from 40,000-90,000, while the Macedonians probably lost something like 1,200 men. While the Persian numbers are likely exaggerated, they could easily be in the tens of thousands since the heaviest losses would have occurred after the battle as the Persians fled the field. Either way, it was a bloody and complete loss for the Persian army, despite a massive numerical advantage, due to Alexander's superior tactical ability, his leadership skills, and the discipline of his soldiers.

At the head of the cavalry, Alexander renewed the chase for Darius, assuming that the Persian king would make for the city of Arbela, which indeed he did. However, night fell before Alexander could reach the city. Upon crossing the Lycus River, he and his men made camp, while Parmenion and the infantry took the remains of the Persian camp, including the baggage train, elephants, and camels.

The End of the Persian Empire

Alexander reached Arbela the next day, but Darius had already continued on, intending to regroup for the next fight. He made for Media, expecting that Alexander would take the easy open roads to the prized cities of Babylon and Susa, while the route to Media was a rough path that would be difficult to traverse with a large army that was unfamiliar with the territory. Much of Bessus's Bactrian cavalry remained with him, as well as some Persian soldiers, the Immortal bodyguards, and many of his Greek mercenaries.[28]

As both Alexander and Darius knew, while Darius was living and free, the war was not yet over, and Darius was certainly persistent and resilient. He made his way to Ecbatana, always staying one step ahead of Alexander, while he attempted to reform his forces to a point that he could again challenge the young conqueror. He had accumulated approximately 3,300 cavalry, 4,000 archers, and 30,000 infantrymen, including the 4,000 Greek mercenaries who remained unswervingly loyal.

---

[27] Chugg, 5.88.
[28] Arrian, 3.16.1–2.

When he left Ecbatana heading in the direction of Bactria, he knew that Alexander was still closely pursuing him and coming closer all the time, as his cavalry detachment moved much quicker than Darius's large force of mixed horsemen and foot soldiers. He therefore called his commanders together to exhort them for a coming battle, telling them, "I have personal experience of both your courage and your loyalty from evidence more compelling than I should have liked, and I ought to strive to prove myself worthy of such friends rather than wonder whether you remain the men you were. Of the many thousands under my command you are the ones who have followed me, twice defeated and twice in flight, and your unflinching loyalty makes me believe that I am a king… Even had I been considering flight (an idea I find thoroughly unacceptable), I would have been encouraged by your bravery to face the enemy. How long, I ask, am I going to be an exile in my own kingdom and flee through my own empire from a foreign king, when by trying the fortunes of war I can either recover what I have lost or else achieve death with honour? …I beg and beseech you: assume the courage appropriate to your reputation and that of your nation to meet whatever fortune has in store for us with the resolute spirit with which you have faced the events of the past. As for me, I shall certainly have perpetual fame conferred on me, whether by a glorious victory or a glorious battle." Darius's oldest friend and closest advisor, Artabazus, spoke up bravely and said, "We shall follow our king into battle, dressed in our richest robes and equipped with our finest armour, mentally prepared to expect victory but also ready to die."[29]

Though the council applauded his words, Nabarzanes and Bessus did not. They had already conspired to overthrow Darius and take him prisoner. They assumed that should Alexander catch them, they could ingratiate themselves to the Macedonian by handing him Darius. Conversely, if they escaped, they could then kill the king and lead the forces themselves. Nabarzanes tried to lay the framework for their plan, suggesting that Darius temporarily give his command and his kingship to Bessus until Alexander was defeated. After that, Bessus could step down, and Darius could take back the throne.

Perhaps not surprisingly, Darius was infuriated and drew his sword on Nabarzanes, but Bessus and his men prevented him from the attack before withdrawing their forces for a secret council. Artabazus managed to calm Darius, reminding him that he needed to be tolerant of stupidity in such a dire situation. Darius eventually listened to him, but still frustrated, he retired to his tent, leaving the camp in a precarious state. Bessus and the Bactrians tried to encourage the Persian soldiers to join them in a mutiny, but the Persians refused to rise against their king, which they considered the very height of impiety. Meanwhile, Patron, the commander of the Greek mercenaries, was fully aware of the discontent brewing and ordered his men to be ready to arm themselves at a moment's notice. Artabazus proved his worth as second-in-command, for throughout the tense hours he toured the camp, encouraging and rallying the Persians, and then managed to convince Darius to come out of his despair and attend to the situation.[30]

---

[29] Curtius, 5.8
[30] Curtius, 5.9.13--7.

Realizing that the Persians would remain loyal, Bessus and Nabarzanes returned to subtle conspiracy. The next morning, they came before Darius, contrite and apologetic, shedding tears and insisting that they had meant no disrespect by their misguided suggestion. Chugg explained, "Their humble pleas moved Darius, who was naturally kindhearted and sincere, not merely to believe their protestations, but even himself to shed a tear."[31] He fully accepted their apologies and returned to planning for another eventual battle with Alexander.

Patron, however, was not convinced. He had his men remain armed and armored on the coming march, and he resolved himself to warn Darius, though he was not permitted in the king's presence without a direct invitation. He therefore rode as close as he dared to Darius's chariot, endeavoring to catch the Persian king's attention. Bessus feared that the Greek had perceived their treachery, so he stayed directly by Darius's side to interfere with the warning.

Eventually, Darius noticed Patron, and when asked if he wished to speak with the king, Patron confirmed that he did, but only in private. Darius knew enough Greek to be able to converse with Patron, so he dismissed all of his attendants and motioned the Greek to speak. Patron reiterated the loyalty of his men and begged Darius to camp among the Greek mercenaries that night for his own protection. Upon further inquiry, Patron revealed his belief that Bessus and Nabarzanes were still plotting against Darius. Though Darius appreciated the gesture and the loyalty of the Greeks, he insisted that he could not abandon his own countrymen, and that "'if his own soldiers did not wish to save him, then his end had come too late.' Despairing of the king's welfare, Patron returned to those over whom he exercised authority, in order to prepare for every trial of loyalty."[32]

Bessus, now convinced that Patron had given away his plot, could not follow through with his desire to murder Darius on the spot for fear of turning the army against him. Instead, he degraded Patron for being a mercenary and called his honesty into question, before calling upon all the gods to witness his own loyalty. His speech only made Darius even more certain of the truth of Patron's words, but he pretended to take Bessus's side.

It made little difference, since Darius was already in a perilous position. The Greeks numbered only 4,000, while those that might possibly be considering treachery were closer to 30,000. Furthermore, if Darius abandoned his own Persians and went to the Greeks, many of those undecided about the plot might see it as a violation of their trust and a justifiable reason to join the conspirators.

In the end, Darius decided he would rather be betrayed as an innocent than deserve it, so he merely remarked to Bessus that "he had as much evidence of Alexander's sense of justice as of his courage, and any who expected a reward for betrayal from him were mistaken – none would be a more severe avenger or punisher of treason than Alexander."[33]

---

[31] Chugg, 6.70
[32] Chugg, 6.72.

At camp that evening, Darius called Artabazus to him and told him of the charges made by Patron. Artabazus urged Darius to take refuge with the Greeks, certain that the Persian ruler would take the advice, but Darius had already despaired of his life, broken by the treachery of his commanders. He embraced Artabazus, and the two exchanged mutual tears at the farewell. Eventually, Darius had to order his attendants to remove Artabazus by force, for he clung to his king and refused to abandon him. Darius had to look away rather than see the grief of his friend.

After spending time in prayer, he ordered his personal attendants and eunuchs to leave him and save themselves, but they remained in the tent until the arrival of Bessus and Nabarzanes, who entered and ordered Darius arrested and bound with golden chains. They put him in a dirty wagon covered in animal skins, and the wagon was driven by men who did not recognize the Persian king in order to keep his presence a secret.

Despite his captivity, Darius was destined to have some vindication, for his assertion that Alexander would despise the treacherous generals would be proven true. Upon encountering deserters and learning of Darius's imprisonment, Alexander and a small force of the most physically fit men in his army tore across the countryside on horseback, intent on catching the Persians. When Bessus and Nabarzanes learned of Alexander's impending arrival, they went to the wagon serving as Darius's prison and tried to convince the king to mount a horse and run with them to escape Alexander. "Darius, however, declared that the gods had come to avenge him and, calling for Alexander's protection, refused to go along with the traitors."[34] In a fury, they speared the king many times and left him for dead in the cart. They also wounded the animals so that they could not carry Darius away.

Alexander and his men came upon the column of fleeing Persians, but though they searched the camp and the throngs of men, they could not find the king. It was by mere chance that a Macedonian named Polystratus eventually came upon the grisly sight. He was overcome with thirst and sought out a spring that the locals had told him about in order to get a drink. Darius's wounded animals had wandered in a painful daze and finally came to a stop in the same valley, moving towards the water, when they finally died of their wounds. Coming across the speared animals, Polystratus was surprised to hear the moans of a man in pain, and upon further investigation, he found the king in the back of the wagon, alone and at the point of death.[35]

Upon Darius's request, Polystratus brought him some water from the stream, and "he then desired that the following message should be given to Alexander: that 'he died without having done him any acts of kindness, but a debtor to him for the greatest, since he had found his feelings towards his mother and children to be those of a prince, not of a foe; that he had been more happy in his enemy than in his relations, for by his enemy life had been granted to his mother and children, but taken from himself by his relatives, to whom he had given both life and

---

[33] Curtius, 5.12.5.
[34] Chugg, 6.74–76.
[35] Curtius 5.13.15–25.

kingdoms; and that such a requital must therefore be made them as his conqueror should please. For himself, that he made the only return to Alexander which he could at the point of death, by praying to the gods above and below, and the powers that protected kings, that the empire of the world might fall to his lot.'"[36]

Some sources indicate that Alexander arrived before Darius had died, received the Persian king's final blessing in person, and swore to Darius that he would avenge his death. Either way, upon seeing the great king of Persia come to such an end, Alexander was grieved to the point of tears. He covered the body with his own cloak and ordered that Darius's body be returned to Persepolis to lie in state, before being honored with a full Persian funeral and laid to rest among his royal ancestors.

Many conquerors have entered Afghanistan with force, but few have been successful, and none would ever describe the region's pacification as easy. Alexander's incursion also came at considerable cost. With his veteran army, he pursued Bessus into Bactria, but even he was unprepared for the difficulties he faced. The natives were hostile to a man, and the terrain was either mountainous (and virtually impassable to all troops but light infantry) or a barren desert with no water or forage. Alexander reconfigured his army for the hostile terrain, shortening the pikes of his phalanx and lightening the armor of his heavy infantry and cavalry, but even that was not enough. For the first time, Alexander faced an enemy who stubbornly refused to be brought to battle. Bessus, who had been at Gaugamela, must have realized that he could never hope to face the relentless Macedonian war machine in open battle, so he decided to play to the strengths of his native Bactrian, Sogdianan and Scythian troops. He employed hit-and-run guerrilla tactics, dispersing his forces across the whole theater of war. Bessus never concentrated them in numbers sufficient for Alexander to pin them down and destroy them, instead striking out at isolated garrisons, baggage and supply convoys, and vulnerable detachments. Flying columns sent out to rescue belabored outposts were often ambushed, and with virtually every local, it seemed, either feeding Bessus's troops information or actively fighting alongside them, Alexander began to lose his temper. It was time for the Bactrians to reap the whirlwind.

Alexander scarcely needed to worry about public opinion with regards to his treatment of the hostile natives, especially where his Macedonian soldiers and generals, who considered them barely human, were concerned. He began to employ pacification by force, which meant entire cities were razed to the ground and their inhabitants sold into slavery, to be rebuilt anew and colonized by veterans of the Macedonian army who were now disabled or too old for service for the most part. These former soldiers were offered large financial incentives to settle in the troubled province. Furthermore, whole regions were depopulated, with their inhabitants either driven out, sold into slavery or killed, and the regions were re-colonized with Persian subjects imported from the more tractable lands to the west. This virtual genocide was accompanied by the foundation of half a dozen cities to help pacify the surrounding lands, including Alexandria

---

[36] Justinus, 11.15.7–13.

on the Jaxartes, and Alexandria Eschate ("The Furthermost") in what is now Tajikistan. At least one of them still stands today and is one of the most important cities in the region: Kandahar.

The prolonged campaign, the miserable weather conditions, the hostile population, and the constant grind of being forced to fight a seemingly invisible enemy while constantly worrying about receiving a knife in the back from supposedly pacified locals began to wear on Alexander's men. The progress of Alexander's conquests, which barring his great sieges had been lightning-fast, slowed to a crawl, and there was no guaranteeing that what had been conquered would actually *stay* conquered.

Dissension and disillusionment, not least with Alexander himself, were rife. Many of Alexander's generals openly advocated turning back to Mesopotamia, if not Macedonia itself, and there was growing concern, openly voiced about Alexander's "going native". He had begun to adopt certain elements of local dress and took the Persian title of *Shahanshah* ("King of Kings"), but what truly soured his generals against him was the adoption of the Persian custom of *proskynesis*. Quite what *proskynesis* was is unclear, but it is certain that it was some form of obeisance, a courtesy that the many Persian generals and courtiers now accompanying Alexander felt obliged to render him as befitted his title of King of Kings.

The Macedonian generals, however, were having none of it. Obeisances were traditionally left to gods alone, and this, coupled with Alexander's previous declaration that he was the son of Zeus-Ammon, was seen as hubris of the highest degree. Tempers frayed, then finally snapped, and at a banquet that year, Alexander infamously took a spear to Cleitus the Black, one of his generals, in a drunken brawl. Cleitus, who had saved Alexander's life at Gaugamela, had insulted Alexander's Persian courtiers, prompting Alexander to rise in fury and run him through. Tortured with remorse, he took to his rooms and did not emerge for days.

THE MURDER OF CLITUS.

Portrait depicting the death of Cleitus, by Andre Castaigne

For Alexander, there was no respite. There were at least two plots to assassinate him during this period, one of which implicated Alexander's general and boyhood friend Philotas, who was also the son of Parmenion. Philotas was executed for his part in the plot and Parmenion, who had been left behind by Alexander at Ectebana, was assassinated to prevent reprisals. A further plot was uncovered later that year, this time involving Alexander's pages and his personal historian, Callisthenes.

Increasingly beset by difficulties, it seemed as though Alexander's entire invasion of Bactria and the adjoining territories might unravel completely, with not even Bessus's betrayal and assassination in 329 BCE serving as respite. When Bessus's own people captured him and turned him over, Alexander reportedly had his nose and ears cut off, which was an ancient Persian custom for punished rebels. Ancient accounts conflict on how Bessus ultimately died, but they all agree that he was tortured in some fashion or another. According to one account, Alexander ordered two trees to be bent together with great force, and Bessus was then bound to both of them. Then the trees were released, and as they sprung back into their natural positions, Bessus's body was torn apart.[37]

THE PUNISHMENT OF BESSUS.

A portrait of Bessus being crucified by Andre Castaigne

If anything, the man who took his place, the Bactrian Spitamenes, was even more resourceful and cunning than his predecessor, and it took an absolutely titanic amount of gold, men, and vicious fighting (including the storming of scores of hill forts in terrain inaccessible to siege engines, during which Alexander received a serious wound) to finally defeat him. After the Battle of Gabai, where Alexander crossed a river on a huge craft in the face of a colossal arrow-storm and annihilated Spitamenes's levies, the Bactrian general was murdered by his own troops.

There was peace at last, but it was an uneasy peace. Alexander knew this, and because he

---

[37] Plutarch, 43.5–7.

intended to press on still further east, he knew he could not leave Bactria in his rear in a state of unrest, as it would compromise his lines of supply and communication, which were already stretched dangerously thin. Accordingly, in 328 BCE he took as a wife the daughter of a powerful local chieftain, Roxana. This union angered many of Alexander's generals, Persian and Macedonian alike. The Macedonians felt that Alexander should marry a girl of noble Macedonian or Greek birth, and saw this as further proof of Alexander's going native. For their part, the Persians, who looked down upon the Afghans as second-class subjects, would have had him marry a girl of Persian royal blood. Alexander ignored them, however, knowing the importance of keeping Bactria compliant, and when he finally marched south and east he was accompanied by thousands of Bactrian and Sogdianan cavalry, implacable foes turned willing allies.

The End of Alexander

Alexander must have been glad to leave Bactria and its adjoining provinces at his back, but his troubles were far from over. Alexander was planning to march onwards, into India, and had made overtures to the wild tribesmen that inhabited the region that is now Pakistan, but he had been abruptly refused. The chieftains of the hill clans who guarded the passes of the mighty Hindu Kush mountains were determined to make a fight of it, secure in the knowledge that the high passes of their domains were virtually unconquerable. Alexander, never one to accept defiance, made his preparations and, in midwinter, a season traditionally reserved for rearmament and regrouping, he began his campaign. The Aspasioi, the Guraeans and the Assakenoi, inhabitants of the rocky valleys of north-western Pakistan, all opposed him, so Alexander destroyed their fortresses one by one, determined to extinguish them. The hill clans were fierce fighters, and each fortress, small though they generally were, was only carried by storm after days of vicious fighting which resulted in grievous losses among the Macedonian ranks. To give an idea of the brutality of this conflict, Alexander himself was seriously wounded twice during two separate sieges, taking a javelin through the shoulder fighting the Aspasioi and then a spear-thrust to the ankle in the assault against the Assakenoi fortress of Massaga. His reprisal was fierce: every fortress of the hill clans that did not surrender him was razed to the ground, and its inhabitants put to the sword, to the last man.

Despite the war-weariness of his veterans and many of his generals, after having vanquished the hill tribes Alexander pressed south and east into the Punjab. There he clashed with the most powerful enemy he had encountered since he had vanquished Darius at Gaugamela, the great Indian ruler Rajah Porus, whose domains included virtually the whole Punjab and who commanded an army tens of thousands strong. Alexander's force came face to face with Porus's army at the Hydaspes River, in 326 BCE Despite Porus's strong defensive position, Alexander succeeded in forcing a crossing. When Porus threw forward his war elephants, the shock element of his force, Alexander's indomitable phalanx proved equal to the task: his men had faced war elephants before, and instead of bracing to resist their charge they opened their ranks, letting the beasts charge through, then encircled them and brought them and their riders down with their pikes. The phalanx then made short work of the lightly armoured Indian infantry, while Alexander's Companion Cavalry and allied horsemen drove the enemy skirmishers and horsemen from the field. Porus was captured still trying to fight, and Alexander was so impressed with his bravery that he made him governor of his previous kingdom, even going so far as to grant him additional lands.

It was also around this time that one of Alexander's oldest and closest companions, the mighty stallion Bucephalus, finally succumbed to the rigours of campaign and died, though it is unclear whether as a result of illness or a wound. Alexander was distraught at his loss as only a true cavalryman who has lived at his mount's side and shared his last morsel of food with him can be, and he ordered a great monument erected to Bucephalus, on the site of which he founded the city of – appropriately – Bucephala. Given the close association between Alexander and his horse, generals from around the world followed Alexander's lead and ensured that they used a favorite horse as well, from Julius Caesar to Robert E. Lee.

A coin from the Seleucid Empire depicting Bucephalus

Some viewed the death of Bucephalus as a sign from the gods that it was time for Alexander to go home, but he persisted on marching ever onwards, despite the fact that his army was exhausted. Many of his veterans had not seen their homes and their loved ones in over a decade, and the lines of supply and communication back to Macedon were stretched so perilously thin that it was unlikely that any reinforcements would be forthcoming. Moreover, Alexander's continual attempts to blend the Hellenistic and Persian cultures together, including the induction of Persian youths into the Companion Cavalry and his personal bodyguards, were souring his

Greek and Macedonian soldiers against him. Finally, upon reaching the Hyphasis River, they could take it no more. They laid down their arms and refused to march another step eastwards.

Alexander raged, begged, entreated, and even threatened, but his soldiers had enough. Further east lay still more powerful Indian kingdoms that would await them on the eastern bank of the mighty river Ganges with hundreds of thousands of cavalry and infantry, and thousands of war elephants and charioteers besides. Alexander flew into a black rage, refusing all visitors for days, but eventually he relented, realizing that no matter how great their love for him might be, he could not persuade his veterans to march further south. After erecting a monument on the Hyphasis River to mark the easternmost edge, he at last turned his army westwards for the first time in almost 10 years.

The way back to Persia was fraught with peril, and Alexander's army suffered grievously. They encountered fierce resistance from local tribes along the Indus, and upon reaching the Persian Gulf Alexander dispatched the majority of his army into Iran, while he himself led a contingent through the desolate wasteland of the Gedrosian Desert, a barren and inhospitable region that virtually decimated his force. In 324 BCE Alexander finally reached the Persian city of Susa, but the grim tally of his men told the tale of the price of glory all too clearly.

The circumstances of Alexander's death are unclear. Certainly there were plenty of ambitious men, even among his inner circle, who might have wanted him dead, yet all of the main historians for Alexander's life discount the possibility of foul play, claiming no poison was used, and slow-acting venom capable of prolonging a man's agony for two weeks seems technologically unviable for the period in question. Perhaps Alexander was simply exhausted. After all, he was a famous binge drinker, like his father, which did little for his health, and he had been on campaign for more than a decade, having sustained at least three serious wounds in the process. Even today scientists and doctors still try to diagnose Alexander based on accounts of his death, naming potential natural causes like malaria, typhoid fever, or meningitis.

Either way, by the time the 32-year-old king was dead, he had conquered most of the civilized world in the West. The young general was able to overwhelm the mighty Achaemenid Empire, which had stood as the most powerful force in the Near East for over 200 years, and gain some of the most ancient and venerated cultures, including Egypt and Babylon. Alexander's conquest of the Persian Empire was not unlike previous wars of conquest in many ways, but the young Macedonian had a vision to spread the benefits of Greek culture to the conquered peoples, an idea that has been referred to as "Hellenism" by modern scholars. Unfortunately for Alexander, his untimely death meant that he was unable to see his vision fulfilled, but some of his top generals made it their duty to spread Hellenism to the east.

As it turned out, that was about all they would peacefully agree on. The circumstances of Alexander's death are unclear, and there were certainly plenty of ambitious men, even among his inner circle, who might have wanted him dead. That said, all of the main historians for

Alexander's life discount the possibility of foul play, claiming no poison was used, and slow-acting venom capable of prolonging a man's agony for two weeks seems technologically unviable for the period in question. Perhaps Alexander was simply exhausted - he was a famous binge drinker, like his father, which did little for his health, and he had been on campaign for more than a decade, having sustained at least three serious wounds in the process. Even today scientists and doctors still try to diagnose Alexander based on accounts of his death, naming potential natural causes like malaria, typhoid fever, or meningitis.

On his deathbed, some historians claim that when he was pressed to name a successor, Alexander muttered that his empire should go "to the strongest." Other sources claim that he passed his signet ring to his general Perdiccas, thereby naming him successor, but whatever his choices were or may have been, they were ignored. Alexander's generals, all of them with the loyalty of their own corps at their backs, would tear each other apart in a vicious internal struggle that lasted almost half a century before four factions emerged victorious: Macedonia, the Seleucid Empire in the east, the Kingdom of Pergamon in Asia Minor, and the Ptolemaic dynasty in Egypt. During the course of these wars, Alexander's only heir, the posthumously born Alexander IV, was murdered, extinguishing his bloodline for ever.

Although it was an incredibly important period in world history, it is sometimes as confusing as it is frustrating for historians because the allegiances of the generals changed constantly and historical sources are often biased in some regards and utterly lacking in others. Although none of these men were able to replicate Alexander the Great's territorial success, a few carved out sizable empires and were able to establish long-lasting political dynasties. Ptolemy I brought Egypt back to a central position of power in the region, and Seleucus I built a strong empire on the ruins of ancient Babylonia, but other generals, such as Perdiccas, were killed early on in the fighting and slipped into relative obscurity.

Some of the Macedonian generals had a significant impact on the region during their lifetimes, but they left no heirs to carry on their political memories. The general Lysimachus won control of Thrace and established a fairly important kingdom in that land, but when he died his successors all turned on and killed each other, effectively ending any potential dynasty. Similarly, Cassander was a Macedonian general who was involved in the Diadochi Wars, and for a time it looked like he was going to be the biggest winner among the Macedonians. Cassander became the king of Macedon, had direct influence over most of southern Greece, and was courted by the other kings and generals in their conflicts against each other.

For a time, Seleucus I and his successors commanded the largest empire in the world as it stretched from the high plains and deserts of what is now Afghanistan in the east to parts of the Levant and Asia Minor in the west. The empire's early kings were strong and shrewd and committed to the ideas of Hellenism as much as holding power and expanding the realm of their empire, but later rulers did not prove as capable. In time, the Seleucid royal house often descended into orgies of violence which were driven by ambitious men and women.

Despite its troubles and its sheer size and scope, the Seleucid Empire lasted for several centuries, and it would not truly reach its end until the heyday of the legendary Roman general Pompey the Great in the 1st century BCE. By establishing notable Greek cities like Antioch, the empire tried with partial success to create a sense of cultural harmony among a giant melting pot, which spanned thousands of miles and incorporated a countless number of ethnicities. Certain groups chafed under the Hellenization more than others, and the Seleucid Empire witnessed a lot of infighting, but it managed to leave an indelible mark on the region that has lasted to this day.

Although Alexander never lived to rule over Egypt, one of his generals, Ptolemy I, did, and it was he who established the last great pharaonic dynasty in Egypt, known as the Ptolemaic Dynasty. Despite the infighting among them, one thing Alexander's generals did agree upon was their Hellenistic culture. Most famously, Ptolemy's line firmly established the Hellenistic culture of the Greeks while ruling over Egypt, and by marrying within their family line, the Ptolemaic pharaohs kept their Hellenistic heritage until the very end of Ptolemy's line, which died with Cleopatra in 30 BCE. Although the Seleucid Empire is less well known, Alexander's general Seleucus was no less successful in "Hellenizing" Persia and parts of Asia Minor. The Greek influence is still readily visible in the region thousands of years later. Anthropologists have found that some of the earliest Buddha statues constructed in India bear an uncanny resemblance to Ancient Greek depictions of Apollo, and local legend has it that the wild olive trees that grow in some regions of Afghanistan sprang from the olive seeds that Macedonian soldiers spat out on the march – not to mention the presence of Balkan features such as red hair and blue eyes among a significant amount of the locals there to this day. Legends of Alexander crop up amid the popular mythology of half the world, and while some among the Persian Empire called him "the accursed", it is now widely believed that the story of the prophet Dhul-Qarnayn ("The Two-Horned One") in the Qur'an is a reference to Alexander.

The Ptolemies gave ancient Egypt an injection of vitality that had not been seen in the Nile Valley for centuries, preserving many aspects of native Egyptian culture while adding their own layer of Hellenic culture. The first few Ptolemaic rulers proved as able as any of their Egyptian predecessors as they worked to make Egypt a first-rate power in the world once again. Unfortunately, these able rulers were followed by a succession of corrupt and greedy kings, more concerned with personal wealth and power than the stability and greatness of their kingdom. Eventually, Ptolemaic Egypt collapsed due to weak rulers, internal social problems, and the rising power of Rome, but before the Ptolemaic Dynasty was extinguished, it proved to be one of the most impressive royal houses in ancient Egyptian history.

The end of the Ptolemies also happened to coincide with the most famous period of Roman history. In the latter 1st century BCE, men like Julius Caesar, Mark Antony, and Octavian participated in two civil wars that would spell the end of the Roman Republic and determine who would become the Roman emperor. In the middle of it all was history's most famous woman, Cleopatra, who famously seduced both Caesar and Antony and thereby positioned herself as one of the most influential people in a world of powerful men. Cleopatra was a legendary figure even to contemporary Romans and the ancient world, and she was a controversial figure who was equally reviled and praised through the years, depicted both as a benevolent ruler and an evil seductress (occasionally at the same time). Over 2,000 years after her death, everything about Cleopatra continues to fascinate people around the world, from her lineage as a Ptolemaic pharaoh, her physical features, the manner in which she seduced Caesar, her departure during the Battle of Actium, and her famous suicide. And despite being one of the most famous figures in history, there is still much mystery surrounding her and the end of the Ptolemies, leading historians and archaeologists scouring Alexandria, Egypt for clues about her life and Egypt's transition to Roman rule.

For his part, Alexander is viewed by most people today as the greatest of all Macedonian kings, if not the greatest figure of the ancient world. There is no doubt his conquests were unrivaled in scope before his time and would not be duplicated for some time afterward, but his legacy should be based on much more than the lands he conquered. After all, as great as Alexander may have been on the battlefield, his actions ultimately led to the decline of the Argead Dynasty and the decline of Macedonian influence in the region.

That said, the Persian Empire had been an undefeatable powerhouse for years, striking terror in the Greeks. Even though they had managed to defend against the two Persian invasions, both were costly for the Greeks and could hardly be called triumphs. The first Persian invasion saw the sacking and destruction of Eretria, while the second sacked Athens and victory only came because the fighting moved to the sea. Thus, when Alexander consistently defeated the Persians, he accomplished something the Greeks before him could only have dreamed of, and in just a few years he had the world's largest empire at his mercy.

Furthermore, while Alexander himself was intrigued by Persian customs and even adopted a number of them himself (whether as a diplomatic means or out of genuine interest), his march across Persia did more to spread Greek culture to the east than it did to bring Persian culture to the West. Despite the infighting among them, one thing Alexander's generals did agree upon was their Hellenistic culture. Most famously, Ptolemy's line firmly established the Hellenistic culture of the Greeks while ruling over Egypt, and by marrying within their family line, the Ptolemaic pharaohs kept their Hellenistic heritage until the very end of Ptolemy's line. Alexander and his successors also succeeded in "Hellenizing" Persia and parts of Asia Minor, and their influence is still readily visible. Anthropologists have found that some of the earliest Buddha statues constructed in India bear an uncanny resemblance to ancient Greek depictions of Apollo

Without Alexander, the fall of the Persian Empire might not have happened for several more centuries, thereby subverting the Hellenistic Era and perhaps even the rise of Rome. The

Hellenistic cities that Alexander founded and the Hellenistic kingdoms established by his successors bore witness to the transformation wrought upon the world by the military genius of one young Macedonian king, proof positive that one individual can - and did - change the world.

Online Resources

Other books about ancient history by Charles River Editors

Other books about the Persian Empires on Amazon

Other books about Gaugamela on Amazon

Bibliography

Anson, Edward M. "Alexander's Hypaspists and the Argyraspids." *Historia: Zeitschrift Für Alte Geschichte*, vol. 30, no. 1, 1981, pp. 117–120.

Arrian, *The Anabasis of Alexander or The History of the Wars and Conquests of Alexander the Great*, Translated by E.J. Chinnock,
https://archive.org/stream/cu31924026460752/cu31924026460752_djvu.txt

Bosworth, A. B., *Conquest and Empire: The Reign of Alexander the Great*, Cambridge: Cambridge University Press, 1988.

Chugg, Andrew, *Concerning Alexander the Great: A Reconstruction of Cleitarchus*, AMC Publications, Kindle Edition.

Devine, A. M. "Grand Tactics at Gaugamela." *Phoenix* 29, no. 4 (1975): 374–85.

Diodorus Siculus, *The Library of History,* translated by C. Bradford Welles,
http://penelope.uchicago.edu/Thayer/e/roman/texts/diodorus_siculus/home.html

Everitt, Anthony, *Alexander the Great: His Life and Mysterious Death,* New York, Random House, 2019.

Freeman, Philip, *Alexander the Great*, Simon & Schuster, 2011.

Griffith, G. T. "Alexander's Generalship at Gaugamela." *The Journal of Hellenic Studies* 67 (1947): 77–89.

Hammond, N. G. L., *The Genius of Alexander the Great*, London: Duckworth, 1998.

Justin(us), Marcus Junianus, *Epitome of the Philippic History of Pompeius Trogus,* translated by Rev. John Shelby Watson,
http://www.forumromanum.org/literature/justin/english/trans9.html

Mercer, Charles, *Alexander the Great*, New Word City, Inc., Kindle Edition.

Plutarch, *Life of Alexander*, translated by John Dryden,
http://classics.mit.edu/Plutarch/alexandr.html

Polyaenus, *Strategems,* translated by R. Shepherd,
http://www.attalus.org/translate/polyaenus4A.html

Polybius, *The Histories,* Loeb Classical Library Edition,
http://penelope.uchicago.edu/Thayer/E/Roman/Texts/Polybius/15*.html

Quintus Curtius Rufus, *The History of Alexander*, Penguin Books Ltd., 1984.

Sekunda, N., *The Army of Alexander the Great*, Oxford: Osprey, 1984

Worthington, Ian, *By the Spear: Philip II, Alexander the Great, and the Rise and Fall of the Macedonian Empire (Ancient Warfare and Civilization)*, Oxford University Press, Kindle Edition.

Xenophon, *On the Cavalry Commander,* http://perseus.uchicago.edu/perseus-cgi/citequery3.pl?dbname=GreekFeb2011&query=Xen.%20Eq.%20mag.&getid=1

Free Books by Charles River Editors

We have brand new titles available for free most days of the week. To see which of our titles are currently free, click on this link.

Discounted Books by Charles River Editors

We have titles at a discount price of just 99 cents everyday. To see which of our titles are currently 99 cents, click on this link.

Printed in Great Britain
by Amazon